STARTING LINE

HOW TO RUN THE CHRISTIAN RACE

By Will Harrub and Brad Harrub, Ph.D.

FOCUS
PRESS

FRANKLIN, TENNESSEE

STARTING LINE

Published by Focus Press, Inc.

© Copyright 2017 Focus Press, Inc.
International Standard Book Number 978-099925570-4
Cover and interior design by: Nick Long
Cover image by: Getty Images
Interior images by: Getty Images

Printed in the United States of America

For information or to order copies of Starting Line, please contact the publisher.

Focus Press, Inc.
625 Bakers Bridge Avenue, Suite 105
Franklin, Tennessee 37067
www.focuspress.org

Library of Congress cataloging in-publication
Will Harrub (1999-)
Brad Harrub (1970-)

Starting Line
Includes Bible References
ISBN: 978-099925570-4
1. Religion   2. Christianity

Dedication

WILL HARRUB

*To my mom and dad who have spent
every minute of my life since the day
I was born trying to help me
get to Heaven. Thank you for the
countless hours you've spent
teaching, helping, and correcting me.
I love you both beyond words.*

BRAD HARRUB

*To Bill Davis. Thank you for taking
the time to open God's Word and
teaching me the Truth. Thank you for
investing time and energy into my
life and showing me what it
really means to bear fruit!*

Acknowledgements

Special thanks first and foremost to Almighty God. We thank Him for knowledge and wisdom and all praise and glory goes to Him. We also thank our family who shared in this project and listened as we yelled corrections and additions across the kitchen. Special thanks to Joe Howell for planting the seed for this book, reminding me of the importance of a book like this one, and being willing to read each chapter. Also thanks to Tonya McRady and Kinsey Scharmahorn for proofing the manuscript. Thanks to those who are bearing fruit and setting an example for others to follow. And thanks to all those who helped instilling God's Word in our lives to make this book possible.

Table of Contents

Introduction

There is really nothing that compares to that incredible feeling of coming up out of the water knowing your sins have been washed away. Oftentimes, friends and family are there to give you hugs and congratulate you on this important decision. On that special "birthday" you are filled with zeal and excitement.

But then what?

After your hair dries and the hugs have all stopped you can oftentimes feel the zeal trickling away. Suddenly, an overwhelming feeling sweeps over you as you realize there is so much to learn. How do you do everything God wants you to do if you do not have a good knowledge and understanding of what He wants you to do? Your zeal can oftentimes turn to frustration as you want to get busy doing things for the Lord, but you don't know exactly what to do or how to do it.

Add to this it can be overwhelming sitting in a Bible class listening to everyone exchange their thoughts about a Bible passage when you can't even locate the Scripture from which they are reading. How can you be a strong warrior for the Lord if you can't even find the specific books or pronounce some of those odd words in the Bible? Not only do you not know who Melchizedek is, the seven-year old in the next pew can pronounce it and his nine year old sister can spell it!

In Matthew 13, Jesus shares the parable of the sower. In this parable He mentions four different types of soil. The soil in these parables is often likened to the hearts of man. Consider the different scenarios Jesus mentions:

1. Seed that fell by the wayside—this is when someone hears the Word of the kingdom but does not understand it. The wicked one comes and snatches away what was sown in his heart.

2. Seed that fell on stony places—this is the person who hears the Word and receives it with joy, yet has no root—and only endures for a while. When tribulation or persecution arises, he stumbles.

3. Seed that fell among thorns—this is the one who hears the word but the cares of the world and the deceitfulness of riches choke the word and he becomes unfruitful.

4. Seed that fell on good ground—this is the person who hears the Word and understands it, and bears fruit!

One of the purposes of this book is to help you become good soil! Our hope is that together we can help you grow roots that will strengthen you to withstand whatever life throws at you. Our prayer is that with the help of this book you will become the good soil Jesus talks about so that you will bear fruit for His kingdom.

This book is meant to help you navigate some of those first steps as you continue to sink your roots in His Word. Keep in mind this book does not have all the answers, and it won't put the information into your brain through osmosis. You will still need to dig into the Bible and learn for yourself what it says. This handy book is simply meant to provide some answers and information to questions that new Christians often ask.

PUTTING ON THE NEW MAN

*"Therefore, if anyone is in Christ, he is a new
creation; old things have passed away;
behold, all things have become new."*

— 2 CORINTHIANS 5:17

Jesus described the journey to Heaven as going through the narrow gate (Matthew 7:13). However, the next verse of that same passage says that in order to get through the narrow gate we must be on the narrow (or difficult) path. Unfortunately, many people view baptism like a flu shot. Their belief is that as long as you have gone under the water, you are covered for the rest of your life. Sadly, this mindset leads many people to never truly repent and make the needed changes they should in their lives.

The Christian life means you are constantly striving to follow and serve Christ. It means you put away old sinful behaviors and strive to be like Him. Paul describes it as putting off the old man and putting on the new man: "But now, you, yourselves are to put off all these: anger, wrath, malice, blasphemy, filthy language out of your mouth. Do not lie to one another, since you have put off the old man with his deeds and have put on the new man who is renewed in knowledge according to the image of Him who created him" (Colossians 3:8-10).

So what does that look like in real life? How does a new Christian "put on the new man"? It means that as you grow and mature in your Christian walk, you will put away things like profanity, lying, and unkindness to others. For some people it may mean you no longer express road rage to those with whom you share the road. For others it may mean you no longer covet the things that other people have and instead learn to be content.

The more you read God's Word, the more of these attributes you will find. There are three places that you can turn to in God's Word that will give you a head start.

1. In Galatians 5:22-23 Paul lists what he calls the fruits of the spirit. These are character traits that all Christians should endeavor to possess and should be constantly trying to "grow" in his or her life. The fruits of the spirit are love, joy, peace, patience, kindness, goodness, faithfulness, gentleness, and self-control.
2. In Matthew 5 you will discover the Beatitudes. These come from Jesus' famous Sermon on the Mount and discuss attributes we should strive to possess.

"Blessed are the poor in spirit, for theirs is the kingdom of Heaven.

Blessed are those who mourn, for they shall be comforted.

Blessed are the meek, for they shall inherit the earth.

Blessed are those who hunger and thirst for righteousness,
for they shall be filled.

Blessed are the merciful, for they shall obtain mercy.

Blessed are the pure in heart, for they shall see God.

Blessed are the peacemakers, for they shall be called sons of God.

Blessed are those who are persecuted for righteousness' sake, for theirs is the
kingdom of Heaven.

Blessed are you when they revile and persecute you, and say all kinds of evil
against you falsely for My sake. Rejoice and be exceedingly glad, for great is
your reward in Heaven, for so they persecuted the prophets who were before you"
(Matthew 5:3-12).

3. 2 Peter 1:5-8 contains a list of ten referred to as the Christian graces. "But also for
this very reason, giving all diligence, add to your faith virtue, to virtue knowledge,
to knowledge self-control, to self control perseverance, to perseverance godliness,
to godliness brotherly kindness, and to brotherly kindness love. For if these things
are yours and abound, you will be neither barren nor unfruitful in the knowledge
of our Lord Jesus Christ."

One of the things you will notice as you read through these passages is that God is
more concerned with issues of the heart rather than physical abilities. What you are

doing by putting on the new man is sharpening your conscience so that your love for Christ will prevent you from pursuing sinful behavior.

Yes, you can memorize Scriptures, but that practice of memorization will not change your heart. You must be willing to repent and change past behavior—putting off the old man and putting on the new. This is an action step that some new Christians never take. Instead, they wander right back into the world and onto the broad way.

Our advice to you is to never stop. Never reach a plateau and think you have arrived. Instead, view each day of your life as the opportunity to do even better—and grow even more Christ-like. The apostle Paul counseled Christians,

> I beseech you therefore, brethren, by the mercies of God, that you present your bodies a living sacrifice, holy, acceptable to God, which is your reasonable service. And do not be conformed to this world, but be transformed by the renewing of your mind, that you may prove what is good and acceptable and the perfect will of God (Romans 12:1-2).

According to Paul in this passage, we are called every single day to present our bodies as a living sacrifice. The definition of sacrifice is "the destruction or surrender of something for the sake of something else." When we make the decision to become a Christian, we are going to have to make a sacrifice. What we're sacrificing is living for ourselves. The majority of the seven billion people living on this planet live only to please themselves and their own earthly desires. When we become a Christian, we must sacrifice that way of life so that we can live to serve our Heavenly Father.

Word of Caution: You will never become fully Christ-like because you are not Him. Even after you have obeyed the Gospel, you will find yourself entangled or ensnared in sin. The writer of Hebrews admonishes, "Therefore we also, since we are surrounded by so great a cloud of witnesses, let us lay aside every weight, and the sin which so easily ensnares [entangles] *us*, and let us run with endurance the race that is set before us" (Hebrews 12:1). Do not let setbacks cause you to throw in the towel.

So what happens when you sin after you are baptized? (And you will...all humans do.) Don't make the mistake of thinking that now that you're in Christ, you will be free from sin. In 1 John 1:7 we read, "But if we walk in the light as He is in the light, we have fellowship with one another, and the blood of Jesus Christ His Son cleanses us from all sin." In the original Greek this passage indicates that He continually cleanses us—meaning His blood covers those sins that we commit after we are baptized. Does that mean we can just go out and live a wild life without any cares? No, of course not. There must be godly sorrow toward those sins—realizing it is sin that separates us from God—and the earnest desire for forgiveness.

You are likely to meet **many** individuals who have been baptized and attend worship on Sunday mornings but they are not striving to change their lives and be more Christ-like. In fact, you will likely meet many apathetic individuals. Do not allow their apathy to become contagious. Just because others are not striving to be more Christ-like does not mean you should just stop. Keep studying. Keep looking for ways to produce fruit. Keep working on your heart. Stay on the narrow path no matter how many people you encounter walking on the broad way. You'll find that a life committed to Him is much more fulfilling than just going through the motions!

One final word of caution – you have just risen from the waters a new man, you are excited and rejoice with your fellow Christians. You want to share the news with your non-Christian or denominational Christian friends and family as well. They may not share in your joy; some may even be offensive to the point of argument and anger. You may be quizzed or tested and you won't have all the right answers. Unfortunately as close relationships become strained instead of strengthened, and you begin to question your newfound faith in order to fit in again. Do not give up and do not be discouraged. Remember, Jesus expected His followers to walk away from their friends and family to follow after Him and His teaching (Matthew 4:18-22).

Verse to Memorize:

"Create in me a clean heart, O God, and renew a steadfast spirit within me" (Psalm 51:10).

OVERVIEW OF THE BIBLE

*"But these are written that you may believe
that Jesus is the Christ, the Son of God, and that
believing you may have life in his name."*

— JOHN 20:31

For most people, the very thought of first picking up the Bible overwhelms them. They haven't read all of it, and much of what they have read they don't understand. They aren't even sure they are reading it correctly.

Let me reassure you—if this is how you feel you are not alone. In Acts 8 we find a guy (an Ethiopian eunuch) reading from Isaiah and not understanding what he is reading. He needed Philip to teach and help him understand what he was reading. You can spend your entire life studying God's Word, and even on the last day of your life you will still learn something you did not know. You can however master some of the basics.

The Bible is composed of two main divisions:

Old Testament		**New Testament**	
(composed of 39 books)		(composed of 27 books)	
Books of Law	5	Gospels	4
Books of History	12	N.T. History	1
Books of Poetry	5	Paul's Letters	13
Books of Major Prophets	5	Other Letters	8
Books of Minor Prophets	12	Prophecy	1

Those Two main divisions can be further broken down into:

Books of Law	**Gospels**
Genesis	Matthew
Exodus	Mark
Leviticus	Luke
Numbers	John
Deuteronomy	

Books of History	**Book of N.T. History**
Joshua	Acts
Judges	
Ruth	**Paul's Letters**
1 & 2 Samuel	Romans
1 & 2 Kings	1 & 2 Corinthians
1 & 2 Chronicles	Galatians
Ezra	Ephesians
Nehemiah	Philippians
Esther	Colossians
	1 & 2 Thessalonians

Books of Poetry
Job
Psalms
Proverbs
Ecclesiastes
Song of Solomon

Books of Major Prophets
Isaiah
Jeremiah
Lamentations
Ezekiel
Daniel

Books of Minor Prophets
Hosea
Joel
Amos
Obadiah
Jonah
Micah
Nahum
Habakkuk
Zephaniah
Haggai
Zechariah
Malachi

1 & 2 Timothy
Titus
Philemon

Other Letters
Hebrews
James
1 & 2 Peter
1, 2, & 3 John
Jude

Book of Prophecy
Revelation

A Short Summary

Let's start with a general overview of what the Bible is all about. Most people view the Bible as having two major divisions—the Old and New Testaments. However, from this day forward you should consider a third division. This third division comes in Genesis 3. Here's why we put a division there. Consider what man's relationship with God was prior to Genesis 3.

God and man were literally together in the Garden! Genesis 3:8 says, "And they heard the sound of the Lord God walking in the garden in the cool of the day, and Adam and his wife hid themselves from the presence of the Lord God among the trees of the garden." Imagine that for a moment—man was literally in the presence of God. There was no death. There was no sin. There was no sickness or disease. There were no tears. Everything was good. Can you even fathom being in that environment and being in the presence of God?

In Genesis 3 we learn that Adam and Eve sinned and shattered that relationship. God cannot be a holy God and be around sin, so Adam and Eve were no longer able to have Him walk around in their presence. The entire rest of the Bible is trying to tell you and I how to get back into that covenant relationship with God—ultimately through Jesus Christ.

In this short "summary" of God's Word we learn of God's love for man. We learn about His holiness. We learn of His desire to be with us. We learn the consequences of sin. Ultimately we learn the solution: Jesus Christ.

A More Complete Summary

Now let's consider a longer summary.

In the Old Testament, God takes a special group of people called the Israelites (who are later called Jews) and gives them laws and commands to purify and set them apart. He provides them with the Ten Commandments and eventually brings them to the Promised Land. He provides them judges and then kings but sadly they turn to idols and pagan gods. God sends special men—prophets—to call His people back to His ways. The Israelites don't listen however, and God allows them to be taken into captivity by foreign nations. The end of the Old Testament closes with the Israelites awaiting the coming Messiah who will bring them victory over sin and death.

The New Testament begins with four accounts of the life of Jesus. These four versions all have different authors, writing to different audiences, each one stressing different points. All four of these books end with the crucifixion of Jesus and His bodily resurrection. The book of Acts picks up as Jesus ascends into Heaven and the New Testament church is started. Acts follows the "acts" of Peter and Paul as they begin their mission to spread the Gospel. (If you are looking for a place to start reading the Bible we would encourage you to read Luke and Acts.) Following Acts, we have Paul's letters to various churches and individuals. Some of these churches received multiple letters from Paul (1 and 2 Corinthians). We also have other letters penned by men like Peter and James. All of these letters help paint the picture of what the church should look like, and what we should be doing in our daily walk for Him. The Bible then ends with John's revelation.

Some people have summed up the message of the Bible like this:

Jesus is coming. (Old Testament)

Jesus is here. (Four Gospels)

Jesus is coming again. (The remainder of the New Testament)

However you look at it, the Bible is a collection of books over a long period of time that details the redemption of man through Jesus Christ.

Twelve Periods of History

In order to get a better understanding of how everything fits in, it is useful to view God's Word in twelve different periods of history (adapted from Wayne Jackson). An understanding of these separate periods will really help you see when specific Biblical events occurred and how they fit into the overall history of the world. The twelve periods are:

1. Creation and a Period of New Beginnings
2. Patriarchal Age
3. Israelite Bondage
4. 40 Years of Wandering
5. Canaan—the Land of Milk and Honey
6. United Kingdom
7. Divided Kingdom
8. Babylonian and Assyrian Captivity
9. The Dark or Silent Years
10. Christ on Earth
11. Formation of the New Church and Expansion of Christianity
12. Admonition to Established Churches

Brief Summary of the 12 Periods:

Creation and the Patriarchal Age—This period covers the Creation account and the initial history of mankind. It includes the accounts of Adam and Eve through the dispersion of people at the Tower of Babel (the first eleven chapters of Genesis). Major events during this period include the Creation (Genesis 1), the fall of man (Genesis 3), the Noahic Flood (Genesis 6-9), and the confusion of languages and dispersion of people (Genesis 11).

Covenant and Establishment of the Chosen People—This period primarily deals with Abram (later changed to Abraham), Isaac, Jacob, and Joseph. In Genesis 12, God makes a promise to Abraham—preparing the way for His Son. Major events during this period include the life of Abraham and his wife Sarah (Genesis 12-18), God's covenant with Abram (Genesis 15), the destruction of Sodom and Gomorrah (Genesis 19), birth of Isaac (Genesis 21), Sarah's death (Genesis 23), Abraham's death (Genesis 25), birth of Jacob and Esau (Genesis 25), Isaac blessing Jacob (Genesis 27), Jacob marrying Rachel (Genesis 29), Joseph being born (Genesis 30), Joseph mistreated by his brothers and sold into slavery (Genesis 37), Joseph's rise to power (Genesis 41), Jacob's journey to Egypt (46), and the death of Joseph (Genesis 50).

Israelite Bondage—This period encompasses when the Israelites were under Egyptian bondage from a new king "who did not know Joseph" (Exodus 1:8). In Exodus 12:40 we learn that this bondage period lasted 430 years. However, there is some controversy as to whether this time period included the patriarchs' sojourn in Canaan (as included in the Septuagint and the Samaritan Pentateuch). Wayne Jackson points out that some contend the bondage period was only 215 years based upon Paul's statement in Galatians 3:16-17 that from the "promise" to the "law" was 430 years. Major events during this period are the birth of Moses (Exodus 2), Moses at the burning bush (Exodus 3), Moses confronting the Pharaoh (Exodus 5), and the twelve plagues (Exodus 7-11).

Wilderness and 40 Years of Wandering—This is the "waiting period" for the second generation of Israelites that will eventually enter the Promised Land. It is during this period that the people were given the Mosaic Law. Having spied out the land of Canaan, the Israelites are scared and refuse to enter. God punishes them and notes:

"According to the number of days in which you spied out the land, forty days, for each day you shall bear your guilt one year, namely forty years, and you shall know My rejection" (Numbers 14:34). Estimates put the Israelites during this time at more than two million people. Major events during this period are the crossing of the Red Sea (Exodus 14), Law of Moses handed down (Exodus 19-31), incident with the golden calf (Exodus

32), covenant renewed (Exodus 34), formation of the Tabernacle (Exodus 35-40), spies sent to Canaan (Numbers 13), Israel refusing to enter Canaan (Numbers 14), and the death sentence delivered to rebellious generation (Numbers 14).

Canaan–the Land of Milk and Honey—The book of Deuteronomy is primarily a series of sermons from Moses to the Israelites prior to them entering the Promised Land. The twelve tribes are given the Promised Land, and they are asked to conquer those currently inhabiting Canaan. It is during this period that they experience a spiritual renewal, as circumcision is reinstituted and Passover is observed. During this period the people divide the land according to tribes and are ruled by judges. Wayne Jackson recorded, "This period of history, of more than three and one half centuries (cf., 1 Kings 6:1), was characterized by four cycles: (a) The people would rebel against Jehovah; (b) The Lord would send an oppressor to punish them; (c) Israel would cry out for deliverance; and (d) God would raise up a judge to overthrow the enemy and free His people" (Jackson, 1986. pg 35). Major events during this period are the entering of Canaan (Joshua 1), destruction of Jericho (Joshua 6), day lengthened for Joshua (Joshua 10), land divided among the tribes (Joshua 13-21), death of Joshua (Judges 2), Gideon called by God (Judges 6), succession of judges (Judges 9-12), birth of Samson (Judges 13), Samson's defeat of the Philistines (Judges 15), Samson and Delilah (Judges 16), and the death of Samson (Judges 16).

United Kingdom—This period in history represents a time of peace that would end in turmoil, as the Israelites sought for a "king" that they might be "like all the nations" (1 Samuel 8:5). The last judge was Samuel. He was followed in succession by kings Saul, David, and Solomon. Solomon's multiple wives played a role in the division of the kingdom. Major events during this period were the birth of Samuel (1 Samuel 1), Israel's demand for a king (1 Samuel 8), Saul chosen to be king (1 Samuel 9), Saul anointed king (1 Samuel 10), Saul rejected as king (1 Samuel 15), David anointed king (1 Samuel 16), David's defeat of Goliath (1 Samuel 17), David sparing Saul the first time (1 Samuel 24), death of Samuel (1 Samuel 25), David sparing Saul a second time (1 Samuel 26), Saul's death (1 Samuel 31), God's covenant with David (2 Samuel 7), David and Bathsheba (2 Samuel 11), death of David's son (2 Samuel 12), Solomon's birth (2 Solomon 12), David naming Solomon king (1 Kings 1), death of David (1 Kings 2), Solomon requesting wisdom (1 Kings 3), Solomon building the temple (1 Kings 6), Ark of Covenant brought into temple (1 Kings 8), Solomon's heart turning from the Lord (1 Kings 11), and the death of Solomon (1 Kings 11).

Divided Kingdom—The split of the United Kingdom occurred under the reign of Rehoboam, the son of Solomon. The ten northern tribes became known as Israel. They had 19 kings, all of which God considered evil. Prophets such as Elijah, Elisha, Amos, and Hosea tried to bring this rebellious group back. They persisted in their evil ways, and in 722 B.C., God gave them up to the Assyrians (after only 213 years). The tribes of Benjamin and Judah became known collectively as the southern kingdom of Judah. They had twenty kings of which only two would be considered good; the rest committed abominable acts. Prophets like Jeremiah, Ezekiel, and Daniel tried to call them to repentance. Ultimately God gave them up to Babylonian captivity in 606 B.C. (after only 349 years).

Babylonian and Assyrian Captivity—It was during this period that people were exiled, the temple was destroyed, and the city of Jerusalem was burned. Wayne Jackson recorded that this occurred during three deportations: (1) There was the "princely" exile in 606 B.C. when men such as Daniel, Shadrach, Meshach, and Abednego were taken away. (2) There was the exile of the "upper class" in 597 B.C. (2 Kings 24:14, 18). (3) There was the general exile in 586 B.C. at which time the temple and city were burned. It was only after Cyrus, the Persian king overtook the Babylonians (538 B.C.) that the Israelites were allowed to return and rebuild in 536 B.C. Three returns are recorded led by Zerubbabel, Ezra, and Nehemiah. Major events during this period would be the fall of Jerusalem (Jeremiah 39), Shadrach, Meshach, and Abednego thrown into the fiery furnace (Daniel 3), Daniel thrown into the lions' den (Daniel 6), and Nehemiah rebuilding the wall (Nehemiah 3-6).

The Dark or Silent Years—This period of approximately 400 years represents the time between the Old and New Testaments. During this period the synagogue system was established. It was also during this era when the Hebrew language was replaced by Aramaic.

Christ on Earth—This period of 33 years records Jesus Christ reign on earth and what he taught His disciples. With His death He nailed the Old Law to the cross (Colossians 2:14; Ephesians 2:15), instituting a new and better covenant. Major events during this period were the birth of Jesus (Matthew 1-2), John baptizing Jesus (Matthew 3), Jesus preaching the Sermon on the Mount (Matthew 5-7), Jesus calling His twelve disciples (Matthew 10), John the Baptist beheaded (Matthew 14), the transfiguration with Peter, James, and John (Matthew 17), the triumphal entry (Matthew 21), Jesus instituting the Lord's Supper (Matthew 26), Jesus tried and crucified (Matthew 26-27), and Jesus risen from the tomb and seen by others (Matthew 28).

Formation of the New Church and Expansion of Christianity—In Acts 2 we find Peter preaching the first Gospel sermon. It was on this occasion, the day of Pentecost, that the church of Christ was established. Wayne Jackson records, "The first century church spans approximately seventy years (from 30 A.D. to 100 A.D.) and may be viewed in the following historical segments: (1) the Jerusalem Church (from the founding of the church on Pentecost to the death of Stephen—five years), (2) the expanding Church (from the death of Stephen to the council at Jerusalem—fifteen years), (3) the Church among to the Gentiles (beginning when Peter preached to Cornelius)(Jackson, 1986, p41-42).

Admonition to Established Churches—The remainder of God's Word represents the closing years. Primarily Paul's letters to various churches, the writing of this period deals with church growth and church conflict. In this period the churches had some of Paul's letters but not the complete Bible. It also represents the transition from a period of miracles to the possession of God's inspired Word.

Verse to Memorize:

"Sanctify them by Your truth. Your word is truth"
 (John 17:17).

THE NEW TESTAMENT CHURCH

"And I also say to you that you are Peter, and on this rock I will build My church and the gates of Hades shall not prevail against it."

— MATTHEW 16:18

Every Sunday morning, church buildings all across our nation are filled with individuals dressed in their very best who have gathered to worship God. They carry their children down the hallway to Bible classes where the children learn the beautiful accounts contained in the Bible—stories such as Sarah and Abraham, Noah and the Flood, Jonah and the big fish, Adam and Eve, Moses and the Red Sea, and Christ and the crucifixion. The adults gather together in Bible classes to study and fellowship with one another. Visitors quickly recognize the genuine love these individuals have for one another, and that visible love helps them to easily make the decision to come back. Following Bible class, the bell rings and hallways fill up with young and old alike, as they slowly file into the auditorium. Within a few minutes, this group blends their voices together in songs of praise, they bow their heads in prayer, and they listen intently to the preacher's sermon. Following the final "amen," this group assembles together in the fellowship hall to eat some of the best home-cooking ever known to touch the tongue. The smell of fried chicken and homemade desserts fills the air, as the fellowship continues.

The scene described above may sound like just an average Sunday morning in "anywhere USA." The portrait contains individuals who maintain perfect attendance, always taking a familiar seat in "their pew." There are guys gathered together to discuss the building and grounds, assigning specific tasks to young, able-bodied men. There are friends who linger long after services to talk and discuss upcoming plans. From all aspects, this appears to be a normal church family—but there is one major difference. While these individuals are sincere in their love for God and their desire to go to Heaven, they are sincerely wrong. They have come up short.

Consider a person who spends his life training for the Olympics. He competes in state and national tournaments and is recognized as the best in his field. If he never gets on a plane and goes to the Olympics then can this person actually declare himself an Olympic athlete? No, he can't—even if he placed first in international competition. He only becomes an Olympic athlete when he makes the Olympic team and then competes in the actual games. Likewise, denominational "believers" may have done many great things, studied the Bible, and believe in Jesus. But the fact remains that they have not learned or obeyed the Truth found in the Word of God. I know this firsthand, because many years ago I was one of them.

Taking Baby Steps Away From Truth *(From Brad)*

Millions of children grow up without any idea that there is one true church that is recorded in Scripture and was founded by Jesus Christ (Colossians 1:18-24; cf. Matthew 16:13-18). Instead, they adhere to the tenets and beliefs of the faith professed by their parents, all the while assuming that they are safe in the arms of God. Their religious identity becomes focused on carrying on the traditions they witnessed while growing up.

These are not sinister people, or people who have purposefully abandoned truth. These are individuals who, in many cases, never had the true seed of God planted in their hearts and minds in the first place. Far too often these individuals leave Biblical education to preachers and older generations—never discovering the truths contained in God's Word for themselves. Sadly, these people epitomize the declaration of the Old Testament prophet Hosea, who boldly asserted "My people are destroyed for lack of knowledge" (Hosea 4:6). A sobering thought remains: How many churches are filled with kind, sincere people who assume the name Christian and expect to spend eternity in Heaven—and yet, they have no real knowledge of what the New Testament teaches?

This was how my spiritual journey began. My parents were both "members" of the United Methodist Church, a denomination founded by John Wesley. I spent every Sunday morning for almost two decades inside a United Methodist Church building. My family was not composed of "CEO" members (Christmas and Easter Only) but rather, we were present every time the doors were open. We attended "Sunday school" each Sunday morning, and gathered both morning and evening for worship. We enjoyed monthly fellowship meals, and proudly helped send missionaries all over the world. From my innocent childhood perspective, we, like so many others in that denomination, were good people who believed in all honesty that we were on our way to Heaven.

Oftentimes denominations incorporate just enough Biblical examples that many are lulled into believing they are in the church described in the New Testament. For instance, many denominations observe the Lord's Supper—but only on a monthly or

These individuals never set out to defy God's divine edicts. They are simply guilty of ignorance.

quarterly basis. Additionally, many baptize members—but few baptize by immersion for the remission of sins. It was with good intentions (but also a lack of Biblical understanding) that my parents had me baptized as an infant. That initial step was later followed up with my "confirmation of faith" as a young teen. From all outward appearances, I was growing up a fine young Christian, but I was not growing up in the Lord. While I spent every Sunday in "church," my biblical knowledge could easily be summed up as lacking at best. Members of the United Methodist Church were encouraged to have daily devotionals and spend time in prayer. However, my experience was that most members believed the preacher would provide any necessary biblical knowledge. Simply put, many individuals did not know the Bible—for I am convinced that if they did know what the New Testament teaches, they would wear the name Christian instead of Methodist. How many sincere people have been led astray by misplaced trust in preachers and lack of their own Biblical knowledge?

I firmly believe that if people would take the time to read the New Testament there would not be as many denominations as we have today.

Man-made traditions and practices that are not mentioned in the Bible can be quickly identified if one has even a basic knowledge of God's Word. It was these man-made traditions and practices that really made me question why the United Methodist Church did certain things. Had I not begun to question the practices and traditions of the United Methodist Church, I probably would still be blindly clinging to its tenets. That truth scares me, and causes me to wonder how many other individuals are blindly walking in the footsteps of their parents.

Incomplete Truth

While denominations expose young people to the concepts of God and Jesus Christ, they often paint an incomplete portrait of who God is, and what He demands. Sermons often describe the loving characteristics of God, and emphasis is placed on salvation by grace and not works. Yet, how often do denominational preachers speak of the wrath or judgment of God, or teach that there is one church—and that Jesus is the head of that church (Ephesians 1: 22-23; 5:23)? How many individuals have placed membership in denominations that possess a central governing body, without giving any thought to the organization set forth in God's Word? How many of these same individuals revere the Ten Commandments, having them posted in Bible classes or in homes—never realizing that Jesus nailed the Old Law to the cross (Colossians 2:13-14; Ephesians 2:14-16).

I firmly believe many of these individuals never set out to defy God's divine edicts. They are simply guilty of ignorance. Far too often our coworkers, neighbors, friends, and even family members believe that religious truths can be found in a "good sermon." They listen to a few verses of Scripture, and conduct themselves in a kind and caring fashion, and assume that they are walking the straight and narrow path as described in the Bible (Matthew 7:14). However, these individuals give no thought as to what actually places someone on that straight and narrow path, and what is required to remain on that pathway. The following information is intended to help individuals find that straight path, and demonstrate the truths contained in the Bible.

Yes, people can be sincere in their love to God, but they can be sincerely wrong. Just a few verses after discussing the broad and narrow gate, Jesus said: "Many will say to Me in that day, 'Lord, Lord, have we not prophesied in Your name, cast out demons in Your name, and done many wonders in Your name?' And then I will declare to them, 'I never knew you; depart from Me, you who practice lawlessness!'" Jesus reminds us that there is a right and a wrong way, and that He will only accept those who obey Him. It is my hope that this book will demonstrate the necessity of planting the seed—which is the Word of God, into the hearts and minds of all those who are lost even if they believer they are on the right path.

Houston, We Have a Problem

Please ask questions! Individuals from any religious background should have the courage to ask questions about the beliefs and organization of their church. If something is indeed accurate, then it can withstand the scrutiny of questions and debate. My original questions regarding the United Methodist Church revolved around many of the traditions and rituals I observed each and every week. For instance, I had frequently participated as an acolyte (a young child who lights candles before worship begins), but I had no idea why this custom was performed or from whence this tradition originated. A close investigation into God's Word quickly reveals that this "position" is not mentioned in the New Testament. And while candles may be aesthetically pleasing to some, we should ask where is the approval for such a practice in the worship setting?

But my questions did not stop there. For instance, week after week our congregation would recite creeds, such as the Apostles' Creed, which states:

I believe in God the Father Almighty, Maker of Heaven and earth. And in Jesus Christ His only Son our Lord; who was conceived by the Holy Ghost, born of the Virgin Mary, suffered under Pontius Pilate, was crucified, dead, and buried; He descended into hell; the third day He rose again from the dead; He ascended into Heaven, and sitteth on the right hand of God the Father Almighty; from thence He shall come to judge the quick and the dead.

I believe in the Holy Ghost; the holy Catholic Church; the communion of saints; the forgiveness of sins; the resurrection of the body; and the life everlasting. Amen.

Each time we uttered these words I would question where this creed came from and why were we stating "I believe in the Holy Ghost, the holy Catholic Church." Also, there was the issue of dramas and skits often performed with the choir singing in the background. Having grown up in the United Methodist Church, I never once questioned the practice of instrumental music. Members of the New Testament church must recognize that for many people in the denominational world, this is not even an "issue." As such, we would frequently sing along with pianos, pipe organs, and occasionally guitars or small bands. Every year our "choir" would perform cantatas or sing along with a dramatized version of the nativity scene. Additionally, our church auditorium (referred to as a sanctuary by those in the United Methodist Church) would routinely have colorful cloths draped over the pulpit and communion table to commemorate specific liturgical seasons (e.g., Lent, Advent, Easter, etc.).

Anyone who is involved in such practices is encouraged to ask questions. Where is the authority for using instruments in worship? Where does the Bible encourage the celebration of Lent or Advent? The more I began to question, the more I realized the United Methodist Church is not founded on the New Testament. The responses I would frequently hear whenever I raised a question is simply: "That's just the way we do it," or "That's tradition," or "I'm not sure why we do that." These answers sent me on a journey to find the Truth.

The Kingdom—the Establishment of the New Testament Church

Each Sunday in the United Methodist Church, we would take pride in our oral rendition of the Lord's Prayer, as members prayed in unison: "Our Father, which art in Heaven, hallowed be thy name. Thy Kingdom come, Thy will be done, on Earth as it is in Heaven. Give us this day our daily bread. And forgive us our trespasses, as we forgive those who trespass against us. And lead us not into temptation, but deliver us from evil. For thine is the kingdom, and the power, and the glory forever. Amen." These words echo the model prayer that Jesus set before His disciples in Matthew 6:9-13. However, many denominational members have never stopped to really consider what they are saying in regards to the kingdom.

The Old Testament prophets revealed that the kingdom (the church) would be established (Isaiah 9:6-7; Daniel 2:44). We learn that the keys of the kingdom were given to Peter as described in Matthew 16:17-19,

> Jesus answered and said to him, "Blessed are you, Simon Bar-Jonah, for flesh and blood has not revealed this to you, but My Father who is in Heaven. And I also say to you that you are Peter, and on this rock I will build My church, and the gates of Hades shall not prevail against it. And I will give you the **keys of the kingdom** of Heaven, and whatever you bind on Earth will be bound in Heaven, and whatever you loose on Earth will be loosed in Heaven" (emp. added).

Furthermore, the Gospel accounts record several occasions on which Jesus and His disciples proclaimed the Kingdom was "at hand." For instance, in Matthew 3:2, John the Baptizer declared: "Repent, for the kingdom of Heaven is at hand" (see also Matthew 4:17; Luke 10:9). These statements indicate that the kingdom would soon be established. *This "Kingdom" is the church.*

Few in the denominational world have ever considered the truths that are found in **Mark 9:1,** where Jesus "said unto them: 'Verily I say unto you, **that there be some of them that stand here, which shall not taste of death, till they have seen the kingdom of God come with power'"** (emp. added, cf. Luke 9:27). This verse teaches that the kingdom would come during the lives of some of those present at that time. Clearly, the kingdom—Christ's church—is already present. Why cling fast to a prayer that is stating "Thy kingdom come"? It is not enough to simply "go through the motions," placing faith in a prayer recorded in the Bible, hoping that this verbal recital will usher them into Heaven. Christians must mentally engage themselves and recognize what God's Word teaches regarding the kingdom.

Founder and Foundation of the Church

Christ, speaking in **Luke 24:46-47,** said: "Thus it is written, and thus it behooved Christ to suffer, and to rise from the dead the third day: And that repentance and remission of sins should be preached in His name among all nations, **beginning at Jerusalem**" (KJV). Quite simply, Christ informs us that the church was to begin in

Jerusalem. Thus, any church that had its origins in America, England, or any other place besides Jerusalem is not **the** church being discussed by Christ. Additionally, after Peter recognized Jesus as the Son of God, Jesus proclaimed: "And I also say to you that you are Peter, and on this rock I will build **My church,** and the gates of Hades shall not prevail against it" (Matthew 16:18, emp. added).

From these two Scriptures alone, we learn that Christ is the founder of His church and it was to begin in Jerusalem. Anyone who is currently occupying a pew in a denomination that does not meet that criterion should boldly ask questions—and seek a church that fits that description. According to the Bible, the head of the church is Christ (Colossians 1:18; Ephesians 1:22-23). As we read about the churches described in the New Testament, it becomes quickly apparent that they were autonomous (1 Peter 5:2). There was no central governing agency here on Earth. The "headquarters" are in Heaven (1 Peter 3:22; Acts 2:29-36). Since this was the original plan that Jesus gave for His church, should not we, as faithful Christians follow that plan?

Church Membership

I can still recall sitting on hard wooden pews listening as the preacher would announce new families who wanted to "join the church." A close inspection of Acts 2 reveals that the notion of "joining a church" is not mentioned in the Bible. We learn in verse 5: "And there were dwelling at Jerusalem Jews, devout men, out of every nation under Heaven"—indicating that the events taking place were occurring in Jerusalem. Verse 41 indicates: "They that gladly received his word were baptized: and the same day there were added unto them about three thousand souls," demonstrating the necessity of baptism. Verses 46-47 inform us: "They, continuing daily with one accord in the temple, and breaking bread from house to house, did eat their meat with gladness and singleness of heart, praising God, and having favor with all the people. And the Lord added to the church daily such as should be saved." Instead of "joining" a church, one should ask if he or she has already been joined (added) to a church!

Concluding Thoughts:

There is no question that there are some denominations that are very entertaining. Some have bands, drama, and even theater lighting. But the question must be asked: Who is the audience of our worship? If it is man, then man gets to decide what he enjoys. If it is God, then the Supreme Creator gets to decide. Rather than attending the one that makes you feel good or is the most entertaining, we should seek out congregations that look and teach like the ones found in the New Testament; the congregations who use God's Word as their foundation.

Verse to Memorize:

"And I also say to you that you are Peter, and on this rock I will build My church and the gates of Hades shall not prevail against it" (Matthew 16:18).

ORGANIZATION OF THE CHURCH

"Let all things be done decently and in order."

— 1 CORINTHIANS 14:40

In the secular world, fancy sounding titles are often easy-to-come-by and hold very little actual value. Sadly, sometimes in religious settings not much thought is given as to whether those titles are Biblical.

For instance, most people have heard a preacher referred to as a "pastor." However, the term "pastor" in the Bible is only used to refer to someone who is serving as an elder and has specific qualifications. Likewise, many denominational preachers use the title "Reverend." The word "reverend" is only found in one place in the Bible (Psalm 111:9), and in that passage it is referring strictly to God. In other words, this special word is used as an attribute of God, and should not be taken lightly. The Catholic religion is known for calling their priests "Father." Yet again, in Matthew 23:9 Jesus said, "And call no man your father on earth, for you have one Father, who is in Heaven." In this passage, Jesus was not referring to a biological father. Instead, He was rebuking the Jewish scribes and Pharisees for rejecting Him and elevating themselves with titles.

Sound confusing? It doesn't need to be. Here is the simple rule of thumb for you to keep in mind: Unless a particular "title" is used in the Bible then do not embrace it within the church. Look for Biblical examples of titles, and then take the next step and look for scriptural examples of the jobs these men performed. An elder is a Biblical position in which one serves as an overseer for a local congregation. Most often elders are not preachers or evangelists; however this is not always the case. Deacons are also mentioned as a position in the church, as well as an evangelist. One important note to remember—we all hold the title of Christian, and as such we are all commanded to walk in the narrow path and teach others.

Elders

Just as a father is to watch over, guard, spiritually feed, and protect his own children, this same concept occurs within a **church family**—with elders acting in the authoritative role. Just as a father corrects and disciplines his children when they are young in order to save their souls, these men perform a similar duty. These are men who care for—and guard—the souls of the entire congregation. This is an enormous role, but one for which you should aspire to. (Even if you do not meet all of the qualifications such as being married with believing children, you can still aspire to conduct yourself like these men do, caring for others.) The Bible indicates that these men "who rule well be counted worthy of double honor" (1 Timothy 5:17) and they will receive a "crown of glory that does not fade away" (1 Peter 5:4).

Historically, elders were ordained in churches once men were qualified. We have examples as the New Testament church was growing in the book of Acts of elders being ordained (see Acts 14:22-23; Acts 20:17; and Titus 1:5). These men—acting as a group—have authority over local congregations (1 Peter 5:2). The Bible indicates they are not to lord this position over the congregation, but rather they are to set an example for the congregation (1 Peter 5:3), and lead the congregation in the direction Christ would have it go. Never forget that Jesus Christ is head of the church (Colossians 1:18; Ephesians 1:22-23). The elders of each congregation must uphold the truths that Jesus has revealed.

Elders go by many names in the New Testament. My favorite is "shepherd" (1 Peter 5:4). This designation implies that the men serving in this capacity are to feed and protect the flock. They are also referred to as Bishops (1 Timothy 3:1-2), Elders (1 Timothy 5:17), Presbyter (1 Timothy 5:1), Pastor (Ephesians 4:11), Overseer (Acts 20:28). Spend a moment truly contemplating what each of these names really means. All of these names reflect the same office, and convey a description of their work. These men play a key role in God's plan for church leadership.

The Bible gives crystal clear qualifications that one should meet to be an elder (1 Timothy 3; Titus 1). One of the biggest mistakes local congregations can make is to install a "good man" who is not truly qualified. It is one thing to understand "business." It is entirely a different thing to have a working knowledge of God's Word and be able to defend it. While many churches use elders to "run" a local congregation and make business decisions, the Scriptures speak of a more important role. If you ever reach the position of an elder, remember that there is a vast difference between gathering around a coffee table with members of your flock versus sitting around a conference table.

Deacons

God in His infinite wisdom designed an office in the church to help meet the needs of members in the local congregation. The specific qualifications for these men can be found in 1 Timothy 3:8-13. These are men who are charged to take care of the physical welfare of the local congregation, which then allows the elders to focus on the spiritual welfare of the congregation. Consider what happens if elders are so busy worrying about building and grounds maintenance or audio/visual issues that they don't have time to consider the spiritual welfare of the congregation. In Acts 6 we see an instance where the widows were being neglected. The Twelve called the disciples together and asked them to select "men of good reputation" (vs. 3) who would allow the apostles to continue studying and praying. Understand that "deacon" is a description—a servant—rather than a title.

Evangelist

In the New Testament the word "gospel" comes from the Greek word "evangelion." One of the best definitions I've heard of this word is to bring joyous news of victory from the battlefield. It is the proclamation of good news! That, in essence, is what an evangelist is supposed to be doing. They are to be proclaiming the "Good News" of Jesus Christ being victorious over the devil and his angels. Preachers are to be evangelists.

Another word that is used in the New Testament to describe this position is minister. Paul observed, "Nevertheless, brethren, I have written more boldly to you on some points, as reminding you, because of the grace given to me by God, that I might be a minister of Jesus Christ to the Gentiles, ministering the gospel of God, that the offering of the Gentiles might be acceptable, sanctified by the Holy Spirit" (Romans 15:15-16).

These words are often used interchangeably. Paul admonished young Timothy, "But you be watchful in all things, endure afflictions, do the work of an evangelist, fulfill your ministry" (2 Timothy 4:5). What was Timothy's ministry? To do the work of an evangelist.

Sadly, I have seen entire congregations split over a preacher. Members oftentimes will get more attached to the man than the church. As a result, anytime there is a change in an evangelist at a local congregation it occasionally results in people leaving and either following him or placing membership with a different congregation. Christians should be converted to Jesus Christ, not a man or congregation.

Some congregations often have enormous expectations for their preacher. In fact, in many congregations the preacher becomes a "pastor" that is in charge of everything. [Note: The term pastor is only used in the Bible to refer to elders. In my example above I am discussing a preacher who is not an elder, but instead he conducts a pastoral system where he is in charge and makes most of the decisions for the congregation.] The role of a pastor and an evangelist differ in both function and qualification. So what does the Bible really say about an evangelist?

Consider for a moment where the church would be if preachers simply dug deeply into God's Word and then stood up and taught that Word to their members each Sunday. Unfortunately, in too many cases, sermons are short on Bible and long on stories, opinions, or jokes. A preacher's primary job is to preach the Word of God.

Preachers in modern times are expected to do a great deal outside of just preaching the Word. In many congregations preachers are expected to counsel, evangelize, visit the sick, do radio programs, print bulletins, perform weddings and funerals, and be present at every church activity. In fact, some members would consider leaving a congregation if the "preacher" didn't visit them in the hospital. But is this what the original writers of the Bible had in mind when they wrote about the role and responsibility of a preacher/evangelist? Shouldn't **all** members be involved in visiting the sick and evangelizing?

Unlike elders who must be married and have believing children, evangelists can be young (see 1 Timothy 4:12), unmarried (like Paul), or without any children. They do not function as shepherds for the local flock. Instead their primary responsibility is to preach the Word. Paul told young Timothy to: " Preach the word! Be ready in season and out of season. Convince, rebuke, exhort, with all longsuffering and teaching" (2 Timothy 4:2). Never forget that. Their primary job is to be in the Word so much that they can effectively communicate that Word to the members of their congregation. When members refuse to evangelize, visit, or teach then it often results in the preacher being pulled away from his primary job.

Preachers can easily fill their days with things like online chat forums, writing blogs, internal programs, or promotional themes/mission statements. However, the result is often shallow sermons that don't contain much from God's Word and ineffective teaching. A weak pulpit will often result in a weak congregation.

Elders have authority to shepherd the flock in local congregations. Evangelists on the other hand have a different type of authority. They are commanded to speak the Word of God with "all authority." In Titus 2:15, Paul admonished, "Speak these things, exhort, and rebuke with all authority. Let no one despise you." When a preacher gets in the pulpit his goal should be to deliver the truths contained in God's Word—and he does so with the authority of God. Any congregation or eldership that asks a preacher not to preach on something that is in the Bible is questioning the authority God has given to preachers. Evangelists are commanded to preach the whole counsel of God (Acts 20:27)—not just the fun and easy verses that make people feel good. What is the job of a preacher? He is to proclaim the victory over the battlefield—that Jesus reigns victorious.

Concluding Thoughts:

It's easy to add a title to someone; what is more difficult is living up to that title. Sometimes titles are given to "good business men" and that is a shame. The Bible gives qualifications for a reason.

Verse to Memorize:

"For the body does not consist of one member but of many" (1 Corinthians 12:14).

ACTS OF WORSHIP

*"And they continued steadfastly in the
apostles' doctrine and fellowship, in the
breaking of bread and in prayers."*

– ACTS 2:42

At this point, you're probably wondering: How can I be sure that a particular congregation is following God's Word? How can I be sure what they're doing is scripturally sound? Thankfully, the New Testament provides instruction for what congregations are supposed to be doing during worship service. Never forget—God is the object and audience of our worship. What we do in a worship setting should be precisely what He has commanded us or shown us through biblical example. In the New Testament we find five different acts of worship that God commands each Christian to participate in. Each one of these is commanded, therefore any congregation who does not do any one of these acts or who adds to them in a way that we don't see in Scripture, is not a scripturally sound congregation. Allow us to give a brief description of each of these five acts of worship:

Prayer

Multiple times in the New Testament, we find passages emphasizing the importance of prayer; not just in our own spiritual lives, but also as an act of worship. In 1 Timothy 2:8, we find Paul telling us, "I desire therefore that the men pray everywhere, lifting up holy hands, without wrath and doubting." In 1 John 5:14, John tells us, "Now this is the confidence we have in Him, that if we ask anything according to His will, He hears us." Prayer is the way in which we talk to our Heavenly Father. If we truly desire to have a relationship with Him, then prayer is something that won't seem like a burden, but rather a privilege. In worship, as a congregation, when you come before the throne of your Heavenly Father, that can be the most spiritually edifying portion of worship service. Think about it for a moment—because we have Jesus as a mediator we can now approach God directly and talk to Him! That should be a powerful thought that should cause you to pause and really think about the importance of prayer.

Our prayer shouldn't just stop after worship concludes however. 1 Thessalonians 5:17, we read, "Pray without ceasing." Just as prayer is an important part of our worship to God, it's also an incredibly important part of our everyday spiritual race. Sadly, many Christians get into a habit of repeating the same words over and over (the Bible warns against these vain repetitions). Don't fall into this rut. Use your prayer to truly open up and talk to your Creator.

Singing

Using our voices to praise God in song is an integral part of our worship to Him. Colossians 3:16 tells us, " Let the word of Christ dwell in you richly in all wisdom, teaching and admonishing one another in psalms and hymns and spiritual songs, singing with grace in your hearts to the Lord." As a new Christian, something you'll notice in your Christian walk is that there are denominations and even some congregations who claim to be churches of Christ, but they will employ the use of instrumental music during worship service. As a New Testament Christian, you will more than likely be questioned as to why you don't use instrumental music. A verse to remember is Ephesians 5:19-20. Writing to Christians, Paul says, "Speaking to one another in psalms and hymns and spiritual songs, singing and making melody in your heart to the Lord, 20 giving thanks always for all things to God the Father in the name of our Lord Jesus Christ." Nowhere in this verse do we see anything about instrumental music.

In fact, out of the 27 books in the New Testament, not a single one of them references any kind of musical instrument being used in worship to God.

Instruments were used in the Old Testament by the Israelites primarily in the temple. After the temple was destroyed, we have no record of followers of God using instrumental music in worship until the 7th or 8th century A.D. It's for these reasons that New Testament Christians don't employ the use of musical instruments in worship. God commands us to sing with our voices and make melody in our hearts. There's nothing that is more spiritually satisfying than sitting with a group of Christians, praising God with our voices. While the world may see the need to use musical instruments, I pray that as a new Christian, you will use the New Testament as your guide. Singing with our voices is commanded by God and is a vital portion of our worship to God.

Teaching

In Acts 20:7, we find that the disciples of Christ met together on the first day of the week and Paul spoke to them a message. Paul's message was probably similar to what you and I call sermons. A sermon or a lesson in worship serves several purposes. First of all, it edifies the members. After a week of living in the world and in the secular

*Joyfully make the time
to praise His name and
thank Him for all your
blessings.*

workforce, it's refreshing to hear a portion of God's word taught to you and in many cases it motivates Christians for the upcoming week. Secondly, it can simply teach the listener. One of the biggest problems in the church today is a lack of biblical knowledge and a sermon during worship service is a great opportunity to build upon the knowledge that you have of God's Word. Finally, a lesson can be used to convict its members of sin in their lives. Sometimes it takes a wake up call from God's Word to draw our attention to sin in our lives that we may need to repent of. Oftentimes, a sermon during worship service causes a pricked heart, which results in repentance from sin. All three of these purposes are reasons why a sermon or an evangelical lesson is commanded as a part of worship.

The Lord's Supper

Observing the Lord's Supper during worship service is a time of intense reflection on the sacrifice Jesus gave for us. In each of the Gospel accounts, right before His crucifixion, Jesus partakes in the Lord's Supper with His apostles and when He does so, he says, "Do this in remembrance of Me." The Lord's Supper is a time in which we fulfill this command given to us by Jesus. 1 Corinthians 11:23-29 gives us a detailed description of what the Lord's Supper is and verses 28-29 inform us that it should be a time of self-examination; a time where we focus on what Jesus did for us on the cross. "But let a man examine himself, and so let him eat of the bread and drink of the cup. For he who eats and drinks in an unworthy manner eats and drinks judgment to himself, not discerning the Lord's body" (1 Corinthians 11:28-29). We encourage you as a new Christian, that when the time comes for the Lord's Supper, to not view it as a habit or as a routine. Instead view it as a memorial and an opportunity we have to remember the incredible sacrifice we've been given. Spend that special time in prayer or reading passages about the crucifixion or reflecting on what Jesus did for you.

Contribution

If you want to get people riled up, then start talking about money. But the reality is everything belongs to God. We are just His stewards. For some reason, Christians sometimes forget that the act of financially giving to the work of the church is an act of worship, but according to Scripture it most certainly is. 1 Corinthians 16:1-2 instructs Christians to lay aside something as we have prospered on the first day of the week. Unfortunately, many baptized believers view this act of worship with dread. When the collection plate comes their way, they feel guilty for not giving, so they give out of compulsion. They give because they feel like they have to. We encourage you personally to never adopt this attitude. 2 Corinthians 9:7 tells us that God loves a cheerful giver. God desires us as Christians to give because we want to, not because we have to. It's not about giving exactly a certain percentage, but rather giving what you decide in your heart (2 Corinthians 9:7). We implore you to give bountifully, rather than sparingly. After all, with all the amazing blessings God has provided us with, why would you not want to return a portion of your blessings to Him?

Concluding Thoughts:

When it comes to worshipping God, we hope you will keep a "get to" attitude. Some individuals view attending worship as "have to." It's something they feel they have to do. Anytime you begin to approach your Christianity with a feeling of "have to," I want you to stop and remind yourself who you are and Who God is (Psalm 46:10). Spend a few minutes in the Psalms to help refresh your memory of the power of our Creator (e.g., Psalm 19). David wrote, "When I consider Your heavens, the work of Your fingers, the moon and the stars, which You have ordained, **what is man that You are mindful of him,** and the son of man that You visit him?" (Psalm 8:3-4, emp. added). When we approach the Church with an attitude of "have to," then it tells me we have forgotten Who God is, how powerful He is, and ultimately what He did for us. How can anyone read John 3:16 and consider attending worship something we "have to" do?

The temptation may arise during your life in which you view your life as important or too busy—and thus church is one more thing you have to fit into your schedule. But remember, without God you would have no life or schedule to fill. Never view worship or spiritual matters with a "have to" attitude. Joyfully make the time to praise His name and thank Him for all your blessings.

THE WORK OF THE CHURCH

"If you love Me, keep My commandments."

— JOHN 14:15

Let's start with the obvious—you cannot work to earn your salvation. The minute you start thinking that somehow good deeds here on earth can earn you a spot in Heaven, you have lost sight of the significance of Jesus Christ and what He did for you on the cross. Our "work" is not to earn salvation, but rather it is to express our love for what He did for us and to fulfill His commands (John 14:15). We work to show our faith to others around us so that God will be glorified and so that others will come to a knowledge of the Truth. James wrote: "But do you want to know, O foolish man, that faith without works is dead? For as the body without the spirit is dead, so faith without works is dead also" (James 2:20,26).

So what exactly is the work of the church and how do you fit into the grand picture? Sadly, some Christians are unemployed and do not feel like they need to work for the Lord's church. Others might be looking for work or living on welfare. In this chapter we want to tell you what the work of the church is and encourage you to become fully employed.

Ask yourself these questions: Why does the church exist? What is the purpose of it? What exactly is the work of the church?

The short answers are:

1. It exists because Jesus Christ founded it on the truth that He is the Son of God and those who believe in Him will be saved.

2. Its purpose is to evangelize the lost and edify the saints.

3. The Bible records three primary areas of work for the church:

    a. Evangelism and Teaching

    b. Benevolence

    c. Edification

Contrary to popular belief, the church is not a building or a location, but rather it's the **people** who make up the church.

"Now you are the body of Christ (the church), and members individually." (1 Corinthians 12:27) The "work" of the church can continue even without a building …

In Genesis 2:15 we read, "Then the Lord God took the man and put him in the garden of Eden to tend and keep it." God has always expected man to work! Jesus said in Mark 13:34, "For the Son of man is as a man taking a far journey, who left his house, and gave authority to his servants, and to every man his work, and commanded the porter to watch." From this statement of Jesus, we learn that the Son of man (Jesus) has taken a far journey (into Heaven), leaving his house (the church), "and to every man his work."

This teaches that there is work to be done in the church. What is your attitude toward work? Unfortunately, in too many cases the church gets "the leftovers" from busy members who give 110% at the office. Consider these questions:

- Do we use our talents as much for the church as we do our secular jobs?
- Do we seek to do our best for tasks at the church or do we just shrug it off as "oh, that's just for the church"?
- Do we brainstorm how we can make things better?
- Do we have a good attitude in doing the work?
- Do you work well with other people to accomplish a common goal of furthering His kingdom?

To better understand the three areas of work in the church, please give serious consideration to the following Scriptures:

Evangelism and Teaching

"Go therefore, and make disciples of all the nations, baptizing them in the name of the Father and of the Son and of the Holy Spirit, teaching them to observe all things that I have commanded you; and lo, I am with you always, even to the end of the age. Amen'" (Matthew 28:19-20).

"And He said to them, 'Go into all the world and preach the gospel to every creature. He who believes and is baptized will be saved; but he who does not believe will be condemned" (Mark 16:15-16).

"Preach the word! Be ready in season and out of season. Convince, rebuke, exhort, with all longsuffering and teaching" (2 Timothy 4:2).

"How then shall they call on Him in whom they have not believed? And how shall they believe in Him of whom they have not heard? And how shall they hear without a preacher?" (Romans 10:14).

"Therefore those who were scattered went everywhere preaching the word" (Acts 8:4).

According to these Scriptures and so many others, we have a responsibility to assist in evangelizing and spreading the Gospel of Jesus Christ. This concept can be incredibly overwhelming at first for new Christians so here's a quick list of practical ways you personally can assist in evangelism:

Practical Ways You Can Evangelize and Teach:
- Talk to friends
- Talk to coworkers
- Get more into the Word than programs
- Add Bible questions to emails
- Use social media
- Have an "open question" to ask strangers about their relationship with Jesus Christ
- Teach Bible classes
- Conduct Bible devotionals in your home
- Invite people to church events

Benevolence – Goodwill or Charity Toward Others

"But now I am going to Jerusalem to minister to the saints. For it pleased those from Macedonia and Achaia to make a certain contribution for the poor among the saints who are in Jerusalem" (Romans 15:25-26).

"and sold their possessions and goods, and divided them among all, as anyone had need" (Acts 2:45).

Now concerning the collection for the saints, as I have given orders to the churches of Galatia, so you must do also: On the first day of the week let each one of you lay something aside, storing up as he may prosper, that there be no collections when I come" (1 Corinthians 16:1-2).

Help the members of the church grow spiritually.

" And let us not grow weary while doing good, for in due season we shall reap if we do not lose heart. Therefore, as we have opportunity, let us do good to all, especially to those who are of the household of faith" (Galatians 6:10).

"Pure and undefiled religion before God and the Father is this: to visit orphans and widows in their trouble, and to keep oneself unspotted from the world" (James 1:27).

"Now in those days, when the number of the disciples was multiplying, there arose a complaint against the Hebrews by the Hellenists, because their widows were neglected in the daily distribution" (Acts 6:1).

Practical ways you can practice benevolence:

- Prepare goodie bags to give out to the poor and panhandlers.
- Find a local organization to get involved with that allows members to see the need firsthand.
- Start or work in a food pantry.
- Begin a food distribution ministry or provide meals to the homeless.
- Look and listen for those who need assistance.

- Visit the shut-ins and widows and take them shopping or to the doctor.
- Assess the needs of your community and set up a means to address it.

Edification

To edify means to build up, to strengthen, to encourage. It is to help the members of the church grow spiritually. What are some of the things that edify? God's Word, fellowship, engaging in worship, helping one another, good works, love, etc.

"Then the churches throughout all Judea, Galilee, and Samaria had peace and were edified. And walking in the fear of the Lord and in the comfort of the Holy Spirit, they were multiplied" (Acts 9:31).

"Therefore let us pursue the things which make for peace and the things by which one may edify another" (Romans 14:19).

"And let us consider one another in order to stir up love and good works, not forsaking the assembling of ourselves together, as is the manner of some, but exhorting one another, and so much the more as you see the Day approaching" (Hebrews 10:24-25).

"Let the word of Christ dwell in you richly in all wisdom, teaching and admonishing one another in psalms and hymns and spiritual songs, singing with grace in your hearts to the Lord" (Colossians 3:16).

Practical ways you can practice edification:

- Have people in your homes and get to know them better!
- Mentor younger people or new Christians.
- Focus more on Christ and spiritual things when you get together rather than just entertainment.
- Have spiritual conversations when you gather together.
- Encourage one another to grow.
- Pray for and with one another.
- Identify one individual in your congregation each week to get to know better.
- Send cards or letters of encouragement.
- Visit those in the hospital from your local congregation.

Concluding Thoughts:

You may not be good at benevolence, but you are great with edification or evangelism. Different people have different talents. Make sure you are using the talents God blessed you with in a way that will glorify Him!

48

YOUR ROLE–CHRISTIAN LIVING

"Do you not know that those who run in a race all run, but one receives the prize? Run in such a way that you may obtain it."

— 1 CORINTHIANS 9:24

Hopefully we've answered many of your questions that are plaguing you in your newfound faith. If you're like many new Christians, however, you're still struggling with some pretty big questions such as, "How do I live my life now that I've become a Christian?" "What's my role as a Christian in everyday life?" "Do I have a responsibility?" These questions are incredibly common so don't feel overwhelmed if you're confused about your role as a Christian. We want to start by giving you a verse that sums up what a Christian's role or responsibility is. In Romans 12:1, we find Paul telling the Romans, "I beseech you therefore, brethren, by the mercies of God, that you present your bodies a living sacrifice, holy, acceptable to God, which is your reasonable service."

This verse perfectly encompasses what a New Testament Christian's role is in everyday living. You see, from the moment you come up out of the water, you are called every single day to make a sacrifice. Sacrifice is defined as, "the surrender or destruction of something prized or desirable for the sake of something considered as having a higher or more pressing claim." To put it more simply, to sacrifice means to give up something valuable to you. So what does Paul mean when he tells the Romans to present themselves as a "living sacrifice?" By using the word "sacrifice," Paul is hitting home the point that being a Christian is not an easy path to take. Making the decision to follow Christ means that more than likely you're going to be placed in uncomfortable positions and maybe even persecuted for your decision. 2 Timothy 3:12 says, "Yes, and all who desire to live godly in Christ Jesus will suffer persecution." God's word virtually guarantees us that living the Christian life will result in persecution. Furthermore, Paul's use of the word "sacrifice" in Romans 12:1 implies that this suffering is voluntary. You see, not only are we going to have to give up comfort, but if we truly desire to follow Christ, we're going to have to give up or sacrifice things like popularity, or certain worldly pleasures. But trust me, the Heavenly reward that we have waiting for us at the end of this life is worth far more than all the pleasure or popularity that this fallen world has to offer. The Christian walk that you have committed yourself to will demand you to make a sacrifice every single day but it will certainly be worth it in the end when we get to spend eternity with our Heavenly Father.

So that's a broad overview of what your responsibility is as a new Christian in everyday life. Now let's get down to some specific responsibilities that you have.

You Have a Responsibility to Attend Worship Service.

What you will notice as you begin your walk as a Christian is that there are many individuals who claim the title "Christian," but they're so nonchalant about attending church that oftentimes you question whether or not they even want to be there. Many times, these individuals attend church once a week, on Sunday morning, and they do it to check it off their list or "punch their religious card" for the week so that any feeling of guilt will be removed. We want to challenge you as a new Christian to strive to avoid this dangerous mindset altogether. Hebrews 10:24-25 reads, "And let us consider one another in order to stir up love and good works, not forsaking the assembling of ourselves together, as is the manner of some, but exhorting one another, and so much the more as you see the Day approaching." There are going to be times where you don't feel like attending worship service. There are going to be times you'd rather rest or watch a football game on Sunday night. But God's Word commands us to meet with other Christians for the purpose of keeping each other accountable and to grow closer to our fellow brothers and sisters in Christ. We implore you as you begin your Christian walk that you make it a priority to never miss a worship service barring sickness or emergency.

You Have a Responsibility to Attempt to Grow Closer to God Every Single Day.

Another dangerous mindset that many individuals who claim to follow Christ employ is the mindset that the only time we're supposed to think about or discuss spiritual topics is within the four walls of a church building. These people come to worship service or a Bible class and then return home often not cracking their Bible open again until the next time they attend worship. Again, we want to challenge you in your walk with Christ to strive to grow closer to God every single day, whether that be through prayer, meditation, or Bible study. 2 Timothy 2:15 reads, "Be diligent to present yourself approved to God, a worker who does not need to be ashamed, rightly dividing the word of truth." You see, after you were baptized you started to form a relationship with God that you'll carry for the rest of your life. Unfortunately, many people allow their relationship with God to grow cold and stale. Oftentimes, this is because their lives become so busy that God gets pushed downward on their list of priorities. As Christians, we must keep God as our ultimate priority no matter how hectic and crazy our lives become.

You Have a Responsibility to Contribute Financially to the Work of the Lord's Church.

This aspect of your role as a new Christian is often one that is responded to with much less vigor than the rest. Nevertheless, as we discussed in chapter five, it's one that is still commanded by God. In 1 Corinthians 16:2, we find Paul telling the Corinthians, "On the first day of the week let each one of you lay something aside, storing up as he may prosper, that there be no collections when I come." Contrary to popular belief, there's nowhere in the Bible that gives instruction on precisely how much of your income you're supposed to give. But we find in 2 Corinthians 9:7 that we're supposed to give cheerfully and not grudgingly. It can be something as simple as setting a certain percentage that you'll give of every paycheck to the work of the church. We encourage you to remember that everything you have belongs to God already, we're simply just returning it back to Him so that His kingdom will continue.

You Have a Responsibility to Assist in Spreading the Gospel of Jesus Christ.

One of the most quoted passages in all of the New Testament is Matthew 28:19-20, which is where Jesus is telling His disciples, "Go therefore and make disciples of all the nations, baptizing them in the name of the Father and of the Son and of the Holy Spirit, teaching them to observe all things that I have commanded you." We encourage you to memorize this passage because it sums up one of your most important roles as a Christian. As baptized believers, we have the most wonderful and life-changing news in the whole world; the news that Jesus died for our sins and rose from the dead so that we could spend eternal life with our Heavenly Father. If we have the solution, the ticket to eternal life with God, why would we not want to share it with anyone and everyone? Whether it be talking to your neighbor, door-knocking with your fellow Christians, or

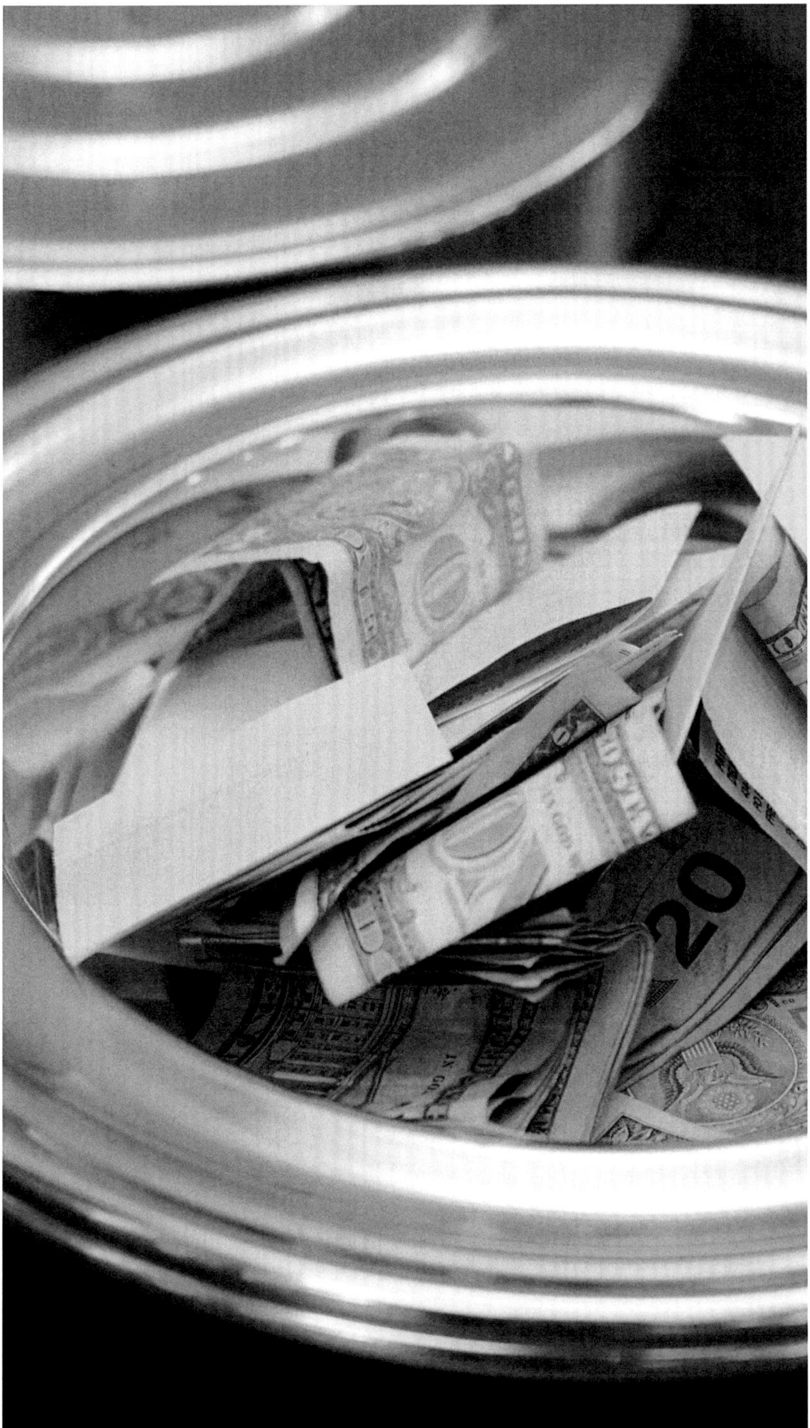

even participating in a mission campaign in a third-world country, we encourage you to count it a privilege and yearn to assist in spreading the Gospel of Christ whenever and wherever you can.

Let Your Actions Preach a Sermon to the World.

The vast majority of people in the United States say they believe in God—but their actions say otherwise. Likewise, those who profess to be Christians recognize that the greatest command is to love God with all of our heart, soul, and mind (Matthew 22:37), and yet, very few demonstrate that kind of love for God. Very rarely does our "love" for God translate into action. Most Christians are comfortable, and will continue to worship and sing praises to God, as long as they don't have to make large sacrifices. We will meet for an hour or two a week, but we are not going to actually give up many of the worldly activities or niceties of life we enjoy. Consider just how much would actually change in many people's lives if they no longer "loved" God. Would anything really change? They would still watch the same television shows, participate in the same activities, and wear the same clothes. This is not the love Jesus was commanding.

This "lukewarm" love (Revelation 3:16) has poisoned the church. In America we have created an environment where God is worshipped in luxurious buildings and we "hire out" our benevolence and evangelism. We have Americanized and sanitized the Gospel so that no one has to get their hands dirty or give up anything. As a result, many hearts have forgotten their first love. The words Jesus quoted from Isaiah should ring in our ears, "These people draw near to Me with their mouth, and honor Me with their lips, but their heart is far from Me" (Matthew 15:8). We say we love God but we refuse to turn our lives over to him as we continue to be a slave to the god of "control." We love God primarily because we feel we should and not because of genuine love that pours deeply out of our hearts, and our children can see it—or a lack of it rather. We think in many Bible classes we learn His precepts and we learn doctrine, but we never teach our children how to establish a relationship with Him.

There is a massive difference between saying you believe in God versus actually forming a relationship with Him. Look at Psalm 63:1-5 and meditate on the picture David paints.

That is what we pray you will have for God—a love that causes you to want to be with Him more than anything. Focus your attention on the greatest command: "You shall love the Lord your God with all your heart, with all your soul, and with all your mind" (Matthew 22:37). We pray your world revolves around Him and your time with Him. Don't allow individuals to Americanize this verse to say, "Love God with all your heart, soul, and mind if it is convenient and does not require sacrifices." Seek a love that will actually change the way you live and cause you to "go upstream" against the apathy we find in many churches today. Some individuals will think that this is radical, and may feel uncomfortable with the thought of it—as it may expose an absence of love for God in their own lives. But we pray that your love for God causes you to turn this world upside down (Acts 17:6)!

In order to establish this type of relationship, you need to start concentrating more on eternity and less on life on earth. Not a day should pass by without you considering Heaven and the fact that this could be the day you meet Jesus! Our love for God should start when we honestly comprehend the magnitude of Who God really is (Isaiah 42:5). If you spend time each day really considering the creative power of God (Psalm 19) and what the Lord has done, your love for Him will grow. How could it not grow when you really consider His creation! We suspect you will find yourself praising God more readily. **Too often individuals look around, and instead of seeing the majesty and awesomeness of God, they see what they don't have.**

Also set aside some time to meditate on the holiness of God (Isaiah 6:3; Revelation 4:8). By focusing on who God is it will become apparent that He cannot have anything to do with sin and still be God. It is virtually impossible to be running the race and pursue God and sin at the same time. Normally you have to stop one to do the other. Focusing on God will help you run toward Him and will leave you less time for sin and trouble. AFinally, take time each day to focus on God's love toward man (John 3:16), and the fact that Jesus conquered death. No matter what comes at you in this life, it pales in comparison to the fact that we can have eternal life with Him. If you do this daily we believe it will prevent what one author deemed "spiritual amnesia."

Notice that these focal points have absolutely nothing to do with you, and everything to do with God. Most people are living their life as though "it's all about me," when the harsh reality is they are just a speck of sand among many in a galaxy too big to fully comprehend. When you begin to focus on God rather than self, your life will soon reflect it. With these eternal thoughts come the realization that many are spiritually dead—and the urgency to teach them about God. That's where our love for God can call us to action.

Some individuals would encourage you to blindly follow the pathway society has set before you and "wait" for God to reveal His plan for you. They find comfort in "waiting" for God. One wonders if these same individuals "wait" to go sporting events, or to go on vacation, or to play golf. We suspect their love of these secular things causes them to act! True love will freely bring about sacrifice and action (1 John 3:16-20). Many of these same individuals are living under the false impression that if they live a good life and are kind, then lost souls will come up and want to know about Jesus. Wrong! Consider for a moment the fact that there are "good" and "kind" lost souls who don't know Jesus. Are people coming up to them as well? Your love for God should cause you to get outside of your comfort zone and tell others about Him.

Real relationships take work and effort. Cultivate the relationship. Spend time with Him. And above all else, love Him with all of your heart!

MAKING MORE FRUIT

"Every tree that does not bear good fruit

is cut down and thrown into the fire.

Therefore by their fruits you will know them."

— MATTHEW 7:19-20

As you start your Christian race you may start to notice that many Christians approach their Christian walk rather apathetically. For a lot of individuals in the church, they come to worship on Sundays and then in their minds they're good to go for the rest of the week. They've mentally checked "Christianity" off their list for the week. What they don't realize is that the word Christian is a verb, not a noun. Rather than just being a label that we wear on Sunday mornings, Christianity is a life that we live. In Matthew 7, we find Jesus explaining to his disciples the danger of false teachers. Take a look at verses 17-20 where He says, "Even so, every good tree bears good fruit, but a bad tree bears bad fruit. A good tree cannot bear bad fruit, nor can a bad tree bear good fruit. Every tree that does not bear good fruit is cut down and thrown into the fire. Therefore by their fruits you will know them."

In this passage, Jesus makes it clear that He will know us by our fruits. If we truly desire to please God by bearing good fruit, then attending worship service and participating in a service project once a month won't be enough for us. We won't want to do the bare minimum. So the question arises, "how do we bear fruit for God's kingdom?" First and foremost you must stay connected to the vine! Your spiritual food, nourishment, and protection should come from Christ. Look at John 15:4-5, "Abide in Me, and I in you. As the branch cannot bear fruit of itself, unless it abides in the vine, neither can you, unless you abide in Me. 'I am the vine, you are the branches. He who abides in Me, and I in him, bears much fruit; for without Me you can do nothing.'" Staying connected to the vine means you continue in prayer, continue to study and meditate on His Word, and live a self-sacrificial life.

Next, you have to look for opportunities to pass on the good news. Someone took the time to share the Gospel with you—or maybe you were raised in a home in which the Gospel was a central theme that you learned. Either way, it's now your turn to bear fruit. God's plan was similar to an apple seed. One apple seed can produce a single apple tree. That apple tree can go on to produce literally thousands of apples during the lifetime of that tree. Someone took the time to plant a single apple seed (you) and now you in turn can produce and plant many more. In other words, you now have the ability to teach the truth to many lost people over the course of your life.

Here are some ways you can bear fruit for God's kingdom:

1. Talk to friends, neighbors, coworkers, and family members about eternal matters.

2. Volunteer to teach Bible classes.

3. Have Bible studies in your home for friends and neighbors.

4. Prepare sermons to preach in your local congregation.

5. Work with the prison ministry in your area.

6. Go door-knocking in your community and share information about the church with neighbors.

7. Write articles or blogs that will help the lost discover the truth.

8. Participate in overseas Bible studies through email or Skype.

9. Mentor someone who is younger.

10. Organize Gospel meetings, VBS, seminars, or revivals for in your community.

This is just a partial list. Your job is to plant seeds. Don't get caught up on how many of those seeds grow—because Jesus reminded us there are four different types of soil. Just keep planting and watering. Eventually, God will give the increase! (Read 1 Corinthians 3:6-9). Remember, your job is not to convert people to a congregation—but rather you are to convert them to the only one who can save them: Jesus Christ.

Welcome to the Starting Line.

Well, here you are as a new Christian. You've just been baptized and you are on fire for God. You are at the spiritual starting line. Everyone who begins the spiritual race begins with fervor and zeal. But as time goes on, as life gets busier, that fervor and zeal dies away. The fire they had inside of them for God starts to flicker. Sadly they start running slower and slower in the race and some even give up altogether. Don't become one of those people. You will probably get tripped up in this race. There will be people who mistreat you along the way. In fact, some of those may even wear the name Christian. The Bible says you will be persecuted. However, in Matthew 10:22 Jesus promised, "And you will be hated by all for My name's sake. But he who endures to the end will be saved."

If you feel tired, worn out, abused, and taken for granted then you are not alone. Paul wrote to Christians in Galatia and cautioned them, "And let us not grow weary while doing good, for in due season we shall reap if we do not lose heart" (Galatians 6:9). These words should be an encouragement to you. Don't forget them.

The race has begun—your race: the Christian race. It is not a quick sprint, but rather it is a life-long marathon. 1 Corinthians 9:24 tells us, "Do you not know that those who run in a race all run, but one receives the prize? Run in such a way that you may obtain it." The prize we're striving for in our spiritual race is not some trophy or medal that can collect dust. Instead, it's the prize of an eternal life with our Heavenly Father. Our prize is Heaven. And when we come to worship simply to check off a box or when we aren't bearing fruit, we're not running in a way that will obtain the prize. Instead we must strive every single day to reach that prize. We have to run that race with zeal from the starting line all the way to the finish line. We pray for each and every one of you reading this book that you will run your spiritual race in such a way that you'll be able to obtain the prize of Heaven. We pray that you will be able to say as Paul did in 2 Timothy 4:7, "I have fought the good fight, I have finished the race, I have kept the faith."

QUESTIONS AND ANSWERS THAT MIGHT HELP YOU

While some of these questions may seem trivial, they are questions that are often asked by new Christians. This is by no means a comprehensive list. Anytime you have a question it is important to see what God's Word has to say on that particular subject instead of relying on your own opinion.

1. Why do we not call the preacher a "pastor?"

In many denominational churches the one who preaches is also called the pastor. However, the Bible reserves the term pastor for someone who is an elder (See Ephesians 4:11; 1 Timothy 3:1-7). It may seem like "nit-picking" but the name actually means something. It comes from the Greek word Poimen and means to tend a flock. It is not the preacher's job to shepherd the flock—that job belongs to the elders. There are specific qualifications for elders that are not the same for a preacher (e.g., married, children, etc.) and as such these terms are not interchangeable.

2. Why do we not call the auditorium the sanctuary?

The word sanctuary means a sacred or holy place. All throughout the book of Exodus it talks about the Sanctuary where God can dwell with the Israelites (Exodus 25:8). Stop and consider for a moment what it means for something to be holy. The place where we come together is not "holy ground." It is merely a meeting place that we have constructed to worship God in the way that He prescribed. We do not read of the 1st Century church meeting for worship in a sanctuary (Acts 2).

3. Why do we have so many translations of the Bible?

Sometimes it can be confusing hearing all the abbreviations for Bible translations (e.g., KJV, ESV, NASB, etc.). When selecting a translation always pick one that has been translated from the original manuscripts and is not a paraphrase. This will ensure you are reading what the original writers actually wrote. There are some good translations that many Christians study from (e.g., NKJV, KJV, ESV, NASB). Many scholars believe the NASB is the most accurate translation—however, it can be hard to read in some instances. The NKJV is also a very accurate translation and is a little easier to read. Some versions are easier to read (e.g., NIV) but they have passages that have been poorly translated. Many Christians will select an accurate translation and then stick with it because it makes memorizing Scripture easier.

4. What about religious holidays?

One of the weirdest transitions you will discover is that New Testament Christians do not celebrate many of the religious holidays that are observed by the world (e.g., Christmas and Easter). It seems weird because this is the one time that the world actually seems to be paying attention to religious things. Do not let that opportunity to speak to others about Christ slip by! Do not be afraid to talk to others during these times. The reason these holidays are not observed is simply this: We are not told to celebrate the birth of Jesus and we observe the Lord's supper every first day of the week! Realistically, we do not know exactly when Jesus was born. December 25th was a day selected by men. Add to this that we are not commanded to celebrate His birth and you begin to understand. Likewise, with Easter we don't know the exact date of the death, burial, and resurrection of Christ. We have been commanded to observe the Lord's supper every first day of the week (See Acts 20:7; Matthew 26:26-29; Acts 2:42; 1 Corinthians 11:23-29). Many Christians do elect to celebrate these holidays as family holidays like Thanksgiving—as a time to enjoy food, family, and friends.

5. Do I have to attend worship on Sunday night?

If you look at it like this then you may have a heart problem. Instead, think about it this way: "You get to!" Part of your job is to transition from the milk of the Word to meat (1 Corinthians 3:2; Hebrews 5:12). You are to continue growing in the faith. How do we do that? Part of it is gathering every time the elders have set aside for us to come together and worship. In Hebrews 10:25 we read, "not forsaking the assembling of ourselves together, as is the manner of some, but exhorting one another, and so much the more as you see the Day approaching." The Bible instructs you not to forsake the assembly. Another way to look at it is this: Jesus Christ should be your first love. If you were newly engaged to someone would you ask "Do I have to go see them?" No! You would want to see them every opportunity you could.

6. Why do we not have female preacher's in the church?

There is a powerful movement that is trying to get females in the pulpit as preachers. Some congregations have already begun using women in leadership roles of worship like leading prayers or leading singing. However, in 1 Corinthians 14:34-35 Paul wrote: "Let your women keep silent in the churches, for they are not permitted to speak; but they are to be submissive, as the law also says. And if they want to learn something, let them ask their own husbands at home; for it is shameful for women to speak in church." Many would argue that this passage was written for their culture at their time, but it is not applicable today. However, look at the reason Paul gave in 1 Timothy 2:11-15, "Let a woman learn in silence with all submission. And I do not permit a woman to teach or to have authority over a man, but to be in silence. For Adam was formed first, then Eve. And Adam was not deceived, but the woman being deceived, fell into transgression. Nevertheless she will be saved in childbearing if they continue in faith, love, and holiness, with self-control." Why did Paul not permit it? Because "Adam was formed first, then Eve. And Adam was not deceived, but the woman being deceived, fell into transgression." Question: Has that changed? Paul's rationale was not cultural or bound by time.

But what if a woman has talents in public speaking or song leading? Consider for a moment that Jesus Christ was a master teacher—and yet, He could not serve as a High Priest. "For He of whom these things are spoken belongs to another tribe, from which no man has officiated at the altar. For it is evident that our Lord arose from Judah, of which tribe Moses spoke nothing concerning priesthood" (Hebrew 7:13-14). Jesus was not permitted to serve as an Israelite priest on earth because of something beyond his control, namely his status at birth. The divine will had decreed that priests were to be appointed from the tribe of Levi through the family of Aaron (Lev. 8:5 ff.; cf. Heb. 7:5), therefore Jesus (of Judah) was not qualified. Did Jesus get mad and demand that He be a High Priest? Or did He humbly submit Himself to the law? We should strive to have the humility and attitude of Christ.

Notes

Notes